PENGUINS

D0089082

Kathleen Weidner Zoehfeld

SCHOLASTIC
REFERENCE

PHOTO CREDITS: Cover: Fritz Polking/Bruce Coleman Inc.; Page 1: Art Wolfe/Photo Researchers, Inc.; 3: John Shaw/Bruce Coleman Inc.; 4: Renee Lynn/Photo Researchers, Inc.; 5: John Shaw/Bruce Coleman Inc.; 6: Fritz Polking/Bruce Coleman Inc.; 7: G. L. Kooyman/Animals Animals; 8: Kjell B. Sandved/Photo Researchers, Inc.; 9: Tom McHugh/Photo Researchers, Inc.; 10: Tom Van Sant/Geosphere Project, Santa Monica/ Science Photo Library/Photo Researchers, Inc.; 11: Bios (Seitre)/Peter Arnold Inc.; 13: Jed Bartlott/Bruce Coleman Inc.; 14: Bios (T. Thomas)/Peter Arnold Inc.; 15: Tui A. DeRoy/Bruce Coleman Inc.; 16: Kevin Schafer/Photo Researchers, Inc.; 17: Dale and Marian Zimmerman; 18: F. Gohier/Photo Researchers, Inc.; 19, 20: Hans Reinhard/Bruce Coleman, Inc.; 21: Bruno P. Zehnder/Peter Arnold Inc.; 22: Kevin Schafer/Peter Arnold Inc.; 23: Art Wolfe/Photo Researchers, Inc.; 24: B. & C. Alexander/Photo Researchers, Inc.; 25: Hans Reinhard/Bruce Coleman Inc.; 26: Art Wolfe/Photo Researchers, Inc.; 27: Hans Reinhard/Bruce Coleman Inc.; 28: Gregory G. Dimijian/Photo Researchers, Inc.; 29: G. L. Kooyman/Animals Animals; 30: Johnny Johnson/Animals Animals.

Library of Congress Cataloging-in-Publication Data available.

ISBN 0-439-42502-6

Book design by Barbara Balch and Kay Petronio
Photo research by Sarah Longacre

10 9 8 7 6 5 4   05 06

Printed in the U.S.A. 23

First trade printing, March 2003

We are grateful to Francie Alexander, reading specialist, and to Adele M. Brodkin, Ph.D., developmental psychologist, for their contributions to the development of this series.

Our thanks also to our ornithological consultant Dr. Dale A. Zimmerman, professor emeritus at Western New Mexico University.

Penguins waddle across ice
and snow on their short legs.

They flop on their bellies
and slide.

They gather onshore or
on big chunks of ice. They
jump into the ocean.

Close-up of an Emperor penguin wing

Penguins are birds. But you will never see them flying in the air.

Penguins have strong, flat wings. They use their wings to swim through the sea.

Stiff tails and big **webbed feet** help them steer.

There are many different
types of penguins. The largest
is the Emperor (**em**-pur-ur).
Emperors can grow as tall as a
six-year-old child.

The smallest penguin is called the Fairy, or Little Blue. Little Blues stand just a little higher than your knee.

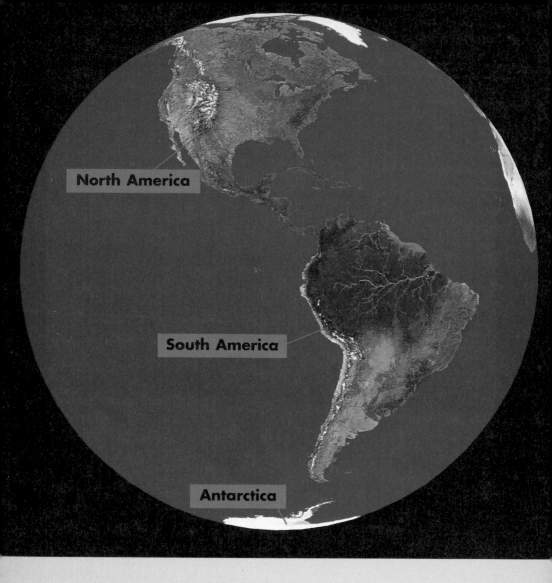

North America

South America

Antarctica

Penguins live only in the
southern half of the world.
Some types live far south, in
the frozen land of **Antarctica**.

All penguins live in places
where the ocean water stays
cold all year long.

Penguins have a thick
coat of small, shiny feathers.
These feathers seal out the cold
water and keep the birds warm
and dry.

For extra warmth, penguins
have a layer of fat, called
blubber, under their skin.

Penguins dive underwater to hunt for fish or for tiny creatures called **krill**.

14

Penguins leap up out of
the water to breathe.

Although they spend most of their lives in the sea, all penguins come onto land or ice to lay their eggs. An area where many penguins lay their eggs is called a **rookery**.

Some types of penguins
build nests of stones and
pebbles on the ground.

Some penguins dig holes
in the ground for their nests.

Others, like the big Emperors, make no nests at all.

Emperors gather together
on the ice. After the mother
penguins lay their eggs, they
are tired and hungry. They
must go back to the sea to feed.

The father penguins stay behind. Each one holds its egg carefully on its feet.

egg

The father penguins huddle close to one another for warmth. They stay together, even through terrible snowstorms. They must keep the eggs warm for many weeks.

When the eggs finally
hatch, the fathers keep the
chicks tucked up against
their snug **brood patches**.

The mothers soon return
from the ocean. Their bellies
are full of krill. They pass the
krill up from their bellies to
feed to their new babies.

In a few weeks, the chicks have grown a warm coat of **downy** feathers.

Penguin parents take turns feeding their fluffy chicks and protecting them.

When a chick's parents are
both away, it can huddle with
other chicks. One or two
adults stay nearby to baby-sit.

After a few months, the
large youngsters begin to lose
their downy feathers.

When their **waterproof**
adult feathers have grown in,
they will be able to take their
first swim. They will catch
their first fish and krill.

The new penguins are
ready for their lifetime home—
the sea!

Glossary

Antarctica—the large area of land around the south pole of the earth

blubber—a layer of fat under the skin of many types of sea animals

brood patches—folds of bare skin on penguins' bellies. Penguins use their brood patches to keep their eggs warm until the chicks hatch

downy—soft and fluffy

krill—tiny, shrimp-like sea animals that gather and swim in huge groups

rookery—a place where a group of birds comes to nest and lay their eggs

waterproof—does not let water pass through

webbed feet—any type of feet with thin, flat folds of skin between the toes

A Note to Parents

Learning to read is such an exciting time in a child's life. You may delight in sharing your favorite fairy tales and picture books with your child.

But don't forget the importance of introducing your child to the world of nonfiction. The ability to read and comprehend factual material will be essential to your child in school, and throughout life. The Scholastic Science Readers™ series was created especially with beginning readers in mind. These books, with their clear texts and beautiful photographs, will help you to share the wonders of science with *your* new reader.

Suggested Activity

You can find penguins on the web site of the Monterey Bay Aquarium. Go to the Splash Zone first. Click on the Penguin Cam to see live videos of penguins. Visit the Focus on Penguins section next. There's lots of fun penguin information here:

www.mbayaq.org

If you live in New York City, you can see penguins in person at the Central Park Wildlife Center. If you live near San Diego, check out the penguins at Sea World of California. Sea World of Ohio, in Aurora, has great penguins. And there are cool penguin exhibits at Orlando's Sea World of Florida, and San Antonio's Sea World of Texas, too.